Robots

By Elizabeth Tyndall

Contents

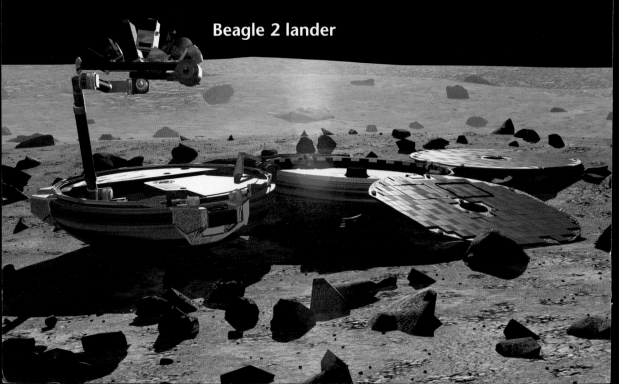

Beagle 2 lander

Robots Around Us

A robot is a machine that works like a human.
It has a computer for a "brain" that allows it to
take instructions. Some robots have **sensors**
that allow them to respond to people
and surroundings.

Robots are found in many places including
factories, hospitals and on farms. They make
life easier for people and help us by doing
dangerous jobs.

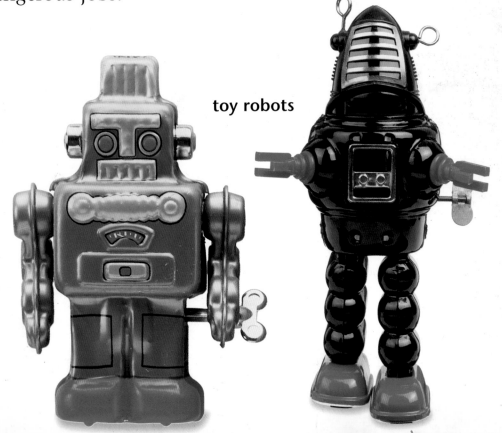

toy robots

Robots Are Unique

Robots are different from other machines.
Most machines need someone to work them.
However, if you **program** a robot, then
it works on its own.

These robots are
being programmed.

Hobo is a robot that
fights fires and works
in dangerous places.

Each robot has a computer called a **controller** for a "brain". This is the part of the robot that is programmed. There are wires that connect the controller to the robot's **motors**. If the controller is programmed with a set of instructions, then it sends electric signals to the motors through wires. Then the motors move the correct parts of the robot.

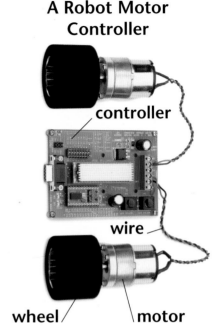

controller

wire

wheel   motor

Remote Control

Robots often work by **remote control**. A robot that works by remote control is called **telerobotic**. Many machines in space are telerobotic such as the Canadarm 2. It receives instructions from scientists on Earth when it is in space.

What Powers Robots

Robots need energy to move. Energy comes from power sources like batteries, solar cells or electricity. Scientists choose different power sources for different reasons.

Rechargeable batteries are a good power source for a robot travelling across the sea. They are carried inside the robot, which is made waterproof to keep them safe. Rechargeable batteries also allow the robot to move freely. However, they run out of power very quickly and often have to be recharged.

ABE is a robot that explores oceans. It runs on large batteries.

This robot, called Sojourner, runs on solar energy. It was built to explore Mars.

Solar energy, or energy from the Sun, is an ideal power source for a robot in outer space. This is because the Sun's energy is unlimited. However, sometimes a planet or boulder blocks the sunlight from reaching the robot. This then cuts off the robot's power and stops it working.

Electricity is useful for powering robots in factories. A robot receives a steady supply of energy when its electrical lead is plugged into the wall socket. However, the electrical lead stops the robot from moving very far.

Electricity provides the power for the robots in this car assembly plant.

Robots on the Move

Over the years scientists have built robots to move in different ways. Early robots moved on wheels. However, this only allowed them to travel over smooth ground.

Then scientists tried to build robots that walked on two legs. But they found it difficult to make the robots balance on their own. As a result, they looked at other ways to make robots move.

In 1865 a walking robot called Steam Man appeared as a character in a book.

A scientist called Rodney Brooks found a new way of making robots move. He noticed that insects balanced well with six legs. So he went away and made the first robot to move like an insect. It had six legs and was called Genghis.

Gyrobot
Gyrobot is a robot on wheels that was built to study balance and movement. It has a device inside that balances the robot as it moves.

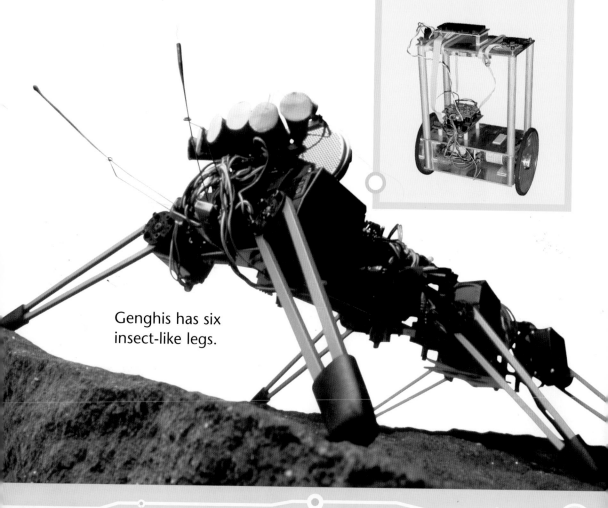

Genghis has six insect-like legs.

Asimo

Asimo walks on two legs. It walks forwards and backwards, turns sideways, goes around corners and walks up and down stairs.

Today robots move in many different ways. They walk, shuffle and gallop. Some even move like fish. Wanda the robot wriggles like a fish. It has flexible skin that allows it to move through the water in many directions.

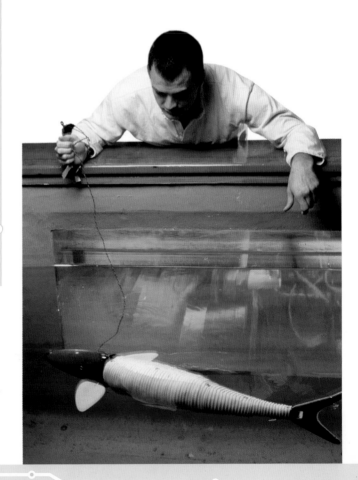

Wanda has flexible skin like a real fish.

Thinking Robots

Now scientists are making robots that "think". These robots solve problems, learn from their mistakes and even respond to people and their surroundings. Robots need **sensors** to "think".

In 2003 World Chess Champion Garry Kasparov and the Deep Junior computer competed against each other.

Elma

Elma is a six-legged robot that can decide where to walk. Sensors in the robot's legs and head help it to walk without bumping into things. Its **controller** allows it to learn from its mistakes. However, Elma forgets everything when it is turned off.

PaPeRo robots use their sensors to move around
a room and to communicate with people.

Robot **sensors** are like a human's five senses.
They gather information about the robot's
environment. They help robots "see" light and
"hear" sound. Pressure sensors let robots tell
whether objects are hard or soft. Built-in
thermometers help them sense heat and cold.

All these sensors let robots make "maps"
of the space around them. Then they can decide
whether or not to follow someone's command.
For example, if a person tells a robot to turn
right and there is a desk in the way, the robot
will ignore the command.

Sensors give robots information about their surroundings. Kismet is a robot head. It senses when a person is too far away or too close. Then it responds by moving closer or farther away. Kismet talks and shows surprise, fear, happiness and anger.

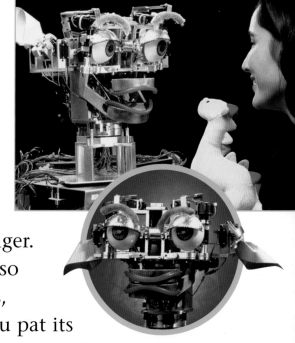

Kismet

Aibo is a robotic dog that also shows emotions. It uses sounds, body language and lights. If you pat its head, then it makes pleasant sounds and lights up. If it is tired, then it lowers its head and slows down. Aibo also sits, shakes hands, fetches balls and barks.

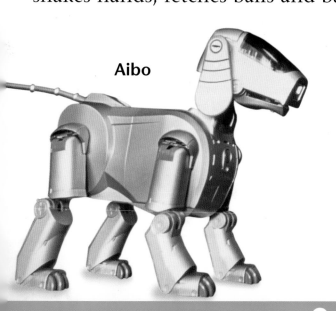

Aibo

Working Robots

Robots are good at doing work. They are especially useful for jobs that are dangerous or boring.

These women are inspecting chocolates made by robots.

Robots in Factories

Robots have been used in factories for many years. They help make all kinds of things from cars to chocolates. Robots can do the same job over and over again without getting tired.

This robotic arm can use a white-hot **welder** without getting too hot or tired.

Robotic Hand

A robotic hand can be made of levers and pulleys. A lever is a long bar that moves at one point. A pulley is a wheel over which a cable runs. The levers and cables are moved by motors controlled by a computer.

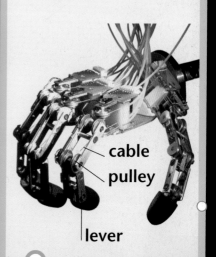

cable

pulley

lever

Robotic arms are often used in factories. These arms have **motors** and cables that make them move. At the end of a robotic arm is an **effector**. This is a tool that is used to do a certain job. It can be a gripper, drill, saw or spray can.

Robots on Farms

Many farms use robots. They make life much easier for farmers. One useful robot is the milking robot. It milks about sixty cows per day.

a milking robot

Another farm robot is the intelligent hoe. It removes weeds growing between rows of crops. A camera on the hoe works with a computer to let the hoe "see" the plants. Scientists are also working on a robot sheepdog that will herd ducks or sheep.

camera

a robot sheepdog

The computer part of the robotic hoe is inside the tractor cab.

Robots in Hospitals

Many hospitals use robots, too. Some robots deliver supplies to doctors. Others push trolleys through the hospital. Robodoc helps in the operating theatre. It drills holes in bones for hip replacements.

Robots help to train medical students, too. Students practise operations on a **simulator** so that they will know what to do when they operate on people.

The HelpMate Robot

HelpMate delivers meals and medicine. It uses **sensors** to guide itself through the hospital. HelpMate is **programmed** to go to any room and to use lifts.

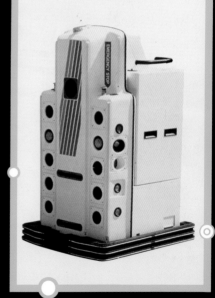

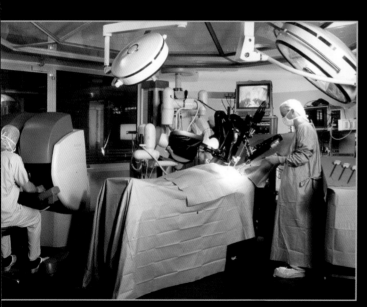

Da Vinci is a robot that helps doctors perform heart surgery.

Robots to the Rescue

Robots do work that is too dangerous for people. Some robots work with bomb squads to disconnect bombs safely. Robot helicopters inspect accidents if fire or fumes make it too dangerous for a pilot.

Robug III has eight legs like a spider and can creep into dangerous places. It can crawl inside a nuclear reactor.

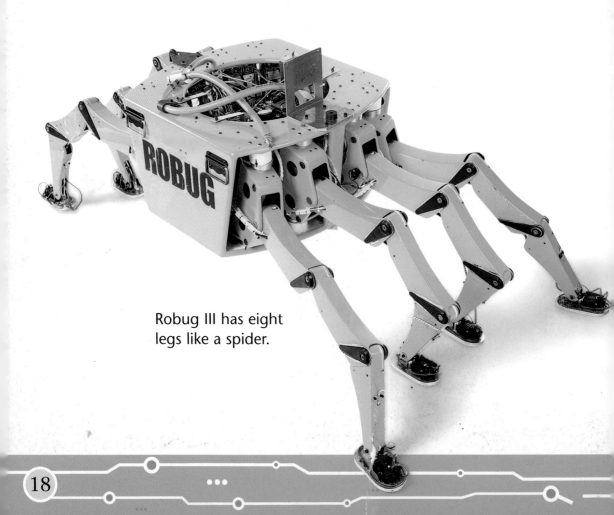

Robug III has eight legs like a spider.

Robot Explorers

Robots are even used in space. They make great space explorers because they don't need air, food or water. They travel to places that are either too far away or too harsh for humans.

In 1999 scientists sent a robot called Stardust to explore a comet. It will collect dust from the comet and return to Earth in about 2006.

Beagle 2
On 2nd June 2003 the European Space Agency (ESA) launched its Mars Express mission. Beagle 2 lander was on board. It was designed to search for signs of life on Mars.

Stardust

Robots are useful under water, too. Humans cannot survive the great water pressure in deep oceans. Scientists send robots to explore instead. Jason Junior is an underwater robot that was used to explore the wreck of the *Titanic*. Jason Junior was connected by cables to another vessel.

Jason Junior took photographs of the inside of the *Titanic*.

Autosub is not connected to a ship. It is powered by **rechargeable batteries** that allow it to move freely. It collects different types of information about life under the sea.

▲ Autosub was launched from the RRS *James Clark Ross* to measure ice thickness in Antarctica.

Autosub is powered by more than 4,700 batteries. ▶

Scientists want to learn more about Earth, but some places are almost impossible for people to explore. Robots like Dante II do these dangerous jobs instead.

In 1994 Dante II inspected a volcano in Alaska. Scientists gave it instructions from a safe distance using **remote control**. The robot climbed up the volcano and returned with important information.

Dante II was built by the National Aeronautics and Space Administration (NASA). They have also built a robot that could walk on Mars one day.

Dante II climbed the Mount Spurr volcano to gather information about the inside of the crater.

Future Robots

Today robots make life easier for many people. Scientists are busy working on new robots for the future. For example, they are trying to develop tiny robots that could operate inside a person.

Maybe someday we will all have robot helpers. Robots might walk our dogs, do our shopping and even help with our homework!

One day you might watch a robot football match with life-size robots.

Glossary

controller	the computer in a robot that is programmed to make it move
effector	the tool at the end of a robotic arm
motors	devices that use energy to make things move
program	to give a machine or robot a set of instructions or codes telling it exactly what to do
rechargeable batteries	energy sources that can be renewed
remote control	a device that gives instructions to a machine from a distance
robotic arms	metal arms that are moved by motors and cables
sensors	parts that get information from the outside world like our eyes and ears do
simulator	a device that allows a person to safely practise skills they would need in a real-life situation
telerobotic	controlled by a person using remote control
welder	a tool that uses heat and sometimes liquid metal to join two metal parts

Index

the Seven Dwarfs robots